Panorama
WESTERN AUSTRALIA

Contents

- 7   Introduction
- 8   South West
- 65   Goldfields & Desert
- 92   Mid West
- 112   Pilbara
- 152   Kimberley
- 191   Acknowledgements

Cover picture: **Bell Gorge in the Kimberley**
Page 1. **Canal Rocks on the Margaret River coast**
Page 2. **Dale Gorge in the Pilbara**
This page: **The Stirling Range**

THE MAP AND REGIONS ABOVE ARE PURELY SCHEMATIC AND DO NOT ADHERE TO ANY TRUE GEOGRAPHICAL OR BOTANICAL ZONING.

Introduction

Once again I take the reader on a panoramic journey through this vast state of Western Australia.

The land is ancient, where the forces of nature for the most part, have changed the surface far slower than many other countries in the world. Testimony to this are, the internal river systems where playa lakes have now formed where once rivers found their way to the sea but now are blocked by later uplifting ranges.

Australia was once part of a super continent but about 140 million years ago, it split away, forming a sub-continent known as Gondwana. In its early stages, it was a very wet and humid island continent, then over the next 50 million years it went through a gradual drying process that has created the unique flora and fauna we know today.

What has always fascinated me is that due to the slow leaching of soils over time, here poor, nutrient deficient soils remain but they support one of the greatest plant species diversity in the world. It truly is one of nature's paradoxes, where poor soils have produced such a great variety of plant life. Plants have adapted to this semi-arid environment by developing their own strategies to cope with continual droughts and fires over the millennia.

This is unlike the northern hemisphere where continual glaciation has literally wiped clean the species numbers and only the more dominant species have remained, hence the lower total of species.

As a naturalist, when I take a photograph, I am often deeply connected to what I'm looking at, as I may know the eucalypt growing in front of me and I will certainly know the species of bird that may be calling. Like the original indigenous peoples of this land, I feel I have a deep connection with the land, brought about by 40 years travelling throughout this vast state.

Why do I still keep producing books, well it's certainly not for financial reward. No, the joy I get roaming this great land allows me to give back to those who may not be able to see some of Western Australia's hidden treasures. A while back, I received an email from a 'Peter' who had my first photographic panorama book. He was very open, and wrote 'Life has been difficult lately but when I'm down, I often open your panorama book and it lifts me up to another place, I thank you for this'. Well how good is that. If I can touch one person's soul, or drag them out of a dark space, it makes it all worthwhile.

You luckily, may not be in a dark space but I hope you too, get some joy from seeing the many areas I have visited and I thank you for supporting a small self-publishing author.

◀ The Old Bakery at Greenhills east of York

South West

The south-west region contains the most diverse habitat types of any region in Western Australia. You can find giant Karri forests, Jarrah forests, limestone sandy beaches, flora rich heaths, high mountains and a lot more. Leaving the temperate wetter forests of the deep south-west, you can pass through the Wheatbelt region with its granite outcrops, rich wildflower reserves, finally coming to the limits of the wheat growing area, what botanists call the Transitional Woodland, a band of eucalypt woodlands that almost encircles the south-west region.

In the wetter region of the south-west, the soils support a lusher vegetation. The tall Karri and Tingle trees tower above the purple hovea and yellow acacia bushes. The undergrowth is thick and it's home to more orchids, fungi and mosses than most of the rest of the state.

It's interesting that compared to the wetter humid regions of the northern hemisphere, the number of species of trees, in our case the eucalypts, is far fewer than even our dryer region, the Western Woodlands, where well over 200 species of eucalypts occur.

The south-west region has been partially cut off from the rest of Australia by the western deserts and this has allowed it to develop many unique plants.

We have car number plates issued by the various states with meaningless statements like 'state of excitement' or the 'smart state', does this mean all the rest are dumb. What Western Australia did have on its plates were the words 'The Wildflower State'. Well it may not have the verbal impact of the others but it certainly is closer to the truth, as there are far more flowering species in the south-west than anywhere else in Australia about 5,600 species to be precise.

The boundary of the south-west region also happens to coincide with the home country of the First Australians here, the Noongar people. Many migrants to these lands have little or no idea of the complex structure of the clan groups that make up the Noongar group. There are 14 clan groups that occur within the boundary of the south-west region, all having similar customs and language and it's wonderful that the Noongar elders are working with linguists to record and write in English vernacular, as there was no written language as stories were passed down through the ages by the spoken word.

Lights Beach near Denmark

▶ **The magnificent coastline north of Margaret River**

Perth

Perth has changed dramatically from when the first European mariners explored these waters. The first European to sail up the Swan River was the Dutchman, Willem de Vlamingh on the 2nd of January 1697. Vlamingh was pretty dismissive of the country but was certainly impressed with his first sightings of Black Swans that he saw in great numbers. When the future first Governor of the new colony, James Stirling sailed in his long boats up the Swan River in March 1827, he was certainly more flattering of the country describing in his diary '…the richness of the soil, the bright foliage of the shrubs, the majesty of the surrounding trees, the abrupt and red-coloured banks of the river occasionally seen and the view of the blue summits of the mountains, from which we are not far distant, made the scenery around this spot as beautiful as anything of the kind I have ever witnessed'. Well from those early days it now supports an expanding, bustling city of nearly two million people and now the fourth most populated city in Australia.

Perth is certainly an isolated city, the nearest town with a population over 100,000 people is Adelaide which is over 2,000 km away and our largest Australian city, Sydney, is further away than Indonesia's capital Jakarta. However, unlike many cities in the world, you don't have to travel far to find peaceful locations to retreat to.

Perth is a fast growing city, for me too fast but as they say that's progress. Luckily, it still is a relatively clean city. There is much for the visitor to see and the Swan River, which meanders to the coast, binds the city together. You can sail on it, travel to Rottenest on it, even catch prawns and fish in it, even see the occasional Dolphin swimming in the estuary.

▶ Matilda Bay

The Narrows Bridge

The Narrows Bridge. In years gone by before dams were built in the Darling Range, the land I am standing on to take this photograph would be submerged when the regular winter floods came down the Swan River.

The first bridge over the Narrows was built in 1959 and was at the time, the largest precast prestressed concrete bridge in the world. With the expansion of the Freeway a mirrored version of the original bridge was built in 2001 and the railway bridge that sits between, was built in 2005 and now services passengers to Mandurah.

Looking across the Swan River from South Perth

Looking across to the Swan River from the Lotterywest Federation Walkway bridge in Kings Park

Kings Park Kings Park is the largest park to be found in any of Australia's large metropolitan cities and it was the early Surveyor General, John Septimus Roe in the mid 1840s who set aside this large 404 ha tract of land above the Swan River. The park was officially opened in 1895 by the first Premier of the State, Sir John Forrest.

Two thirds of the park remains in its natural state but set aside are 18 hectares for the wonderful Western Australian Botanic Gardens, where nearly 3,000 of the unique plant species have been propagated. Plants of the different botanic bio zones of the State have been planted in their respective areas. In the height of spring from late August to early November, the Botanic Gardens are a blaze of colour and the resident gardeners do a phenomenal job keeping so many species alive and some are extremely rare in their natural environment.

Fremantle Harbour

Sugar Loaf Rock This much photographed rock off the Margaret River coast, thrusts its way above the sea line in dramatic style.

It's here that a stunning seabird the Red-tailed Tropicbird in some years makes its most southerly nesting site. It is unusual in as much that the bird is really a lover of tropical waters and nests as far north as Christmas Island. A lone bird that roams the high seas returning to its breeding site to mate and nest.

Their nuptial flight is one of the most spectacular as they fly high tumbling and turning together.

The sun sets at Wyadup Beach north of Margaret River   Between Cape Naturaliste in the north to Cape Leeuwin in the south, in the lower south-west region of Western Australia lie some of the most beautiful beaches in the State. Close by, are some of the finest vineyards, eateries and galleries in Australia. Some parts of Western Australia are backward in presenting a professional front for the visitor to Western Australia but Margaret River, Dunsborough and the Augusta region certainly serve the State very well.

Goblin Swamp west of Pemberton

Beedelup Falls near Pemberton

▶ After sunset on Lake Dumbleyung in the central Wheatbelt

Lake Dumbleyung

The early European settlers had heard from the indigenous inhabitants that a large inland sea existed in the inner wheatbelt region. Henry Landor and Henry Maxwell Lefroy in 1843, decided to make a journey east exploring lands that no European had seen before. On the 17th January, they came across the largest of the inland lakes they had yet seen on their exploration. It was Lake Dumbleyung some 13 kilometres long. The local Wilman tribe of the south-west Noongars called it 'dambelling' meaning large lake. It is the largest body of water in the south-west when it is full.

On this same lake, just over 100 years later on the 31st December 1964, the British speed fanatic Donald Campbell broke the world water speed record on lake Dumbleyung, travelling at a speed of 444.66 km per hr or 276 miles per hr whichever measurement you relate to. He and his crew had arrived at the Lake on the 13th December and the following day was perfect for a record attempt but just as he was about to start it was relayed back that large rafts of ducks had descended on the lake and turbo jet engines don't take kindly to the occasional duck being sucked into the intake barrel, so it was postponed. Several days followed with hot drying winds stirring up the lake. Campbell was finally going to give it up when on the last day, the winds suddenly died down and Campbell made two runs both times breaking the world record.

Campbell was an amazing man and in that same year, he had just broken the land speed record on Lake Eyre in South Australia. Donald tragically died in 1967 on Coniston Water in England trying yet again to break the world water speed record in his famed Bluebird K7. It broke the world speed record moments before Campbell radioed back to his team at 160 km/h 'Passing close to Peel Island, tramping like mad, full house'. At 320 km/h he radioed 'The waters very bad indeed... I can not get over the top'. At 480 km/h 'I'm getting a lot of bloody row in here....I can't see anything'. At 500 km/h it was a new world record. At 460 km/h 'I've got the bows out ...' then sadly his last words '...I'm going'. The boat back flipped and landed at full force on its back and sank. His body and the boat were retrieved many years later. Both Donald and his father Sir Malcolm Campbell broke 21 world speed records, 11 on water and 10 on land, a phenomenal record.

Another famous gentleman also visited Dumbleyung and that was Sir Peter Scott the keen British ornithologist, whose father was the explorer Scott of Antarctic fame. Peter was looking for the attractive Pink-eared Duck, which he managed to see with the help of a local teacher. The only world duck species that Peter never got to find was the elusive Australian Freckled Duck which occasionally can be found in the south-eastern part of the Lake in good years, its stronghold are the ephemeral lakes in the desert regions but occasionally when the deserts are in drought, these ducks can be seen in Perth, particularly at Herdsman Lake.

▲ **Pink-eared Duck**
▶ **Freckled Duck**

Fitzgerald River National Park

This large park is a botanist's dream and a camper's delight with so much to see in this park between Albany and Esperance. The photograph is certainly not an award winning image but I include it, as in the foreground on the left is the beautiful and very restricted endemic plant the Barrens Regelia. It epitomizes the relationship between certain soil types and specific plant species that only grow in certain soils. Here the East Mt Barren range is covered in quartzite rocks. While I was wandering over a less impressive low range of hills just north of Moora, I noticed another beautiful flowering Regelia and looking down at my feet the ground was covered in quartz. It was certainly a different species but showed that the same genus of plant loved growing amongst these sharp fragmented stones.

The Fitzgerald supports over 1600 flowering species, 62 being found nowhere else outside the park. The largest genus in the park are the eucalypts with approximately 80 species, that's quite incredible for a park just 85 kms long. It also holds the greatest variety of banksias of any park in WA.

We often read that an area has the most this or that compared with other areas in the world and we can become desensitised to facts but it still is amazing that a park can contain over 1600 species of plant life which is over a quarter of the total species for the whole of the south-west region, and so it is one of the botanical hotspots in the world.

Dotted along the Fitzgerald coast both east and west are some lovely camping grounds that generally do not get the high visitor numbers like the parks adjacent to Perth and one can get here within a day from Perth, so there's ample opportunity to have un-pressured time.

▲ The flower is commonly known as the Quaalup Bell

◄ Fitzgerald River National Park looking down to West Beach from East Mt Barren

The Stirling Range

Named by John Septimus Roe, the first Surveyor General after the first Governor of the state James Stirling. Roe wrote in his diary *'The Stirling Range burst on our view in great magnificence as we rounded the crest, the whole extent of the conical summits were spread before us'*.

This beautiful range of hills looks even more impressive than many Australian mountain ranges, due to the fact that the general surrounding country is generally flat and being a relatively young range, the peaks have been forced up dramatically due to the collisions of Gondwana and the Antarctic continents.

Many people mistakenly think that Bluff Knoll is Western Australia's highest peak but Mount Meharry in the Pilbara is the tallest followed closely by another Hamersley Range mountain Mount Bruce.

The rocks of the Stirling Range consist mostly of sedimentary rocks that were once ancient seabeds are now thrust skywards. These rocks consist of sandstone, quartzite (altered sandstone) and shales laid down in these early oceans and the ripples of the receding waters on the ancient sands and examples of fossils can now be found high up on the mountain tops. On the high slopes of Bluff Knoll (Noongar name – Koikyennuruff), there is still an abundance of flowering species. Some of the restricted mountain bells of the Darwinia genus can be found on Bluff Knoll. In the lower part of the range, the Stirling Range Banksia along with the Giant Andersonia lower down in the western part of the park is a rare banksia and growing and close by the beautiful Cranbrook Bell.

Over a third of the total number of flowering plants in the south-west grow in this park and to put it in perspective, that's more than the total count for the British Isles.

The park is best visited between August and early November. If you come in late November, many of the flowers will not be in bloom. You will not be disappointed if you come in mid-September, particularly if earlier in spring you have travelled in the Mulga region and there have been no everlastings to see due to a dry season. Here in the Stirling Range, even if the year has been relatively dry, there will always be some species in flower.

For the bushwalkers and mountain climbers there are many great walks one can take but start early if you intend to climb in the summer.

▲ The red flower is a Scarlet Banksia and the beautiful star like flower is the very sort after Queen of Sheba orchid.

Granite outcrops

If you look at a map of the primary bedrocks on a geological map of Australia, the ancient Archaean Yilgarn Craton not only dominates the interior of south-west Australia but also dominates all of Australia as a single mass of granite bedrock.

Here in the south-west and also in the Pilbara, lie some of the most ancient rocks on earth, the only older granites are those that are found in Canada. These outcrops mainly consist of granite-gneiss metamorphic rock and greenstone, laid down over 2800 mya. All of eastern Australia was yet to be formed, that's how old the western region is. If you are in Perth and look across the sedimentary coastal plain to the Darling Range where the granite protrudes through the laterite mantle, you are looking at almost the youngest and oldest landforms in one view.

Capping this massive Yilgarn Craton is a mantle of varying rocks and soil types that have been deposited by different drainage systems and marine deposits. Over time, with constant weathering

by wind and rain and leaching, these hard bedrock granites and quartz rocks, have been exposed as massive domes and boulders.

They tower above the surrounding wheatbelt plains. In my Parks book on Western Australia, I photographed and detailed 37 of the major outcrops that occur in the wheatbelt, such is my love for these ancient rock islands and I have always gravitated to them, not just to photograph but as is phrase that is often loosely quoted, it gives me a 'sense of place'. It certainly gave the first Australians a sense of place, for below many of these outcrops there are soaks or gnamma holes that gave life saving waters.

Many plants can be found just on or at the base of granite outcrops. One plant, the Sandpaper Wattle grows in the gravel debris that is found at the base of some granite outcrops, particularly those in the north-eastern Wheatbelt.

▲ **Billiburning Rock north of Beacon**

◀ **Looking over Baladgie Lake from Baladgie Rock west of Bullfinch**

◀ **Sand Paper Wattle**

BUSHFIRE: *the ever present danger that Australia has to sometimes face.*

Behind the trees that are silhouetted against the skyline is a raging bush fire that has taken out thousands of acres. The colours you see opposite have not been altered by any Photoshop technique, they are real. I found the colours produced during the fire almost surrealistic and the photographs over the page have been taken close by.

I once had a 100 acre bush block near the Stirling Range containing beautiful mature Wandoo trees with patches of species-rich heath. There were 32 species of orchid within the confines of my block. I had just finished moving into a new building that I had built for visiting naturalists, mainly bird watchers. Above my study window a pair of Carnaby's Black-Cockatoo nested in the hollow of a giant Wandoo tree. It was paradise for me but life throws things at you that are out of your control. It was a hot December day, the temperature at 9.30 am was 35 degrees and I knew it was a potential fire day and as it turned out it certainly was. The fire started just north of the small township of Tenterden. Within a short period it was bearing down on my property. Even though I was surrounded by open woodland that could pose a fire risk, I had a 10 metre clear gravelled buffer zone around the house with a full sprinkler system in place on the roof, run by a separate fire-fighting pump.

Before the main fire-wall engulfed the property, the wandoo trees started to catch alight as ash from a few kilometres away were falling from the sky and igniting the trees. At that stage I turned off my fire-fighting hose and went inside to brace for the main fire-wall. When it came, it was like listening to 20 roaring trains coming at you. The fire jumped over the house and kept on going. I was told it reached speeds of 70 kilometres an hour. After it had passed, I tried to open the sliding glass doors but the radiant heat was too much.

◀ **Fire on the Williams – Collie Road**

When I finally could go outside all the trees were alight but miraculously my house was saved but the bush block was almost like a burnt desert with all the trees alight. My dream was literally up in smoke. Life can be tough but at least I was alive, alas for two Tenterden ladies it was not to be.

The south-west part of WA is particularly a fire prone area and this is mainly due to the fact that the climate is a Mediterranean-type climate, having long hot dry summers combined with the presence of highly combustible vegetation, particularly the eucalypts and proteaceae plants which can be very combustible. Over time, many plants have adapted to fire, some use the process of 'serotiny' which allows seeds stored in the soil, to germinate when affected by fire or heavy smoke. Hakea seeds for example hold their seed until the fire has passed through and the seeds pop out into the fertile ash and re-sprout over the following months.

▲On the Williams-Collie Road. The fire and smoke with low light created this amazing contrast between fire smoke and the brightly lit paddocks.

▼On the Williams – Collie Road

Tutanning Nature Reserve

Tutanning Nature reserve east of the small town of Pingelly, is one of the most flora rich areas in the central Wheatbelt, containing many rare plants. To put it into perspective, a botanist in the early 1900s collected over 400 species for the British Museum from the reserve and that's long before we had the introduction of extensive taxonomic classification revision, so imagine the number of species now. Certainly with time things change, even in my own life-time I have seen the demise of the Mallee Fowl from this reserve and I think the Tammar Wallabies are in trouble. Luckily Tutanning Reserve still supports an incredible wealth of plant life. Thank heavens the feral fox and cat do not eat our valuable flora like they do our small reptiles and mammals.

The profusion of species illustrated in this photograph is the result of the after growth from a fire in the sheoak woodland in the reserve. A smaller photograph taken mid-summer highlights the amazing changes between the seasons and you can still see the blackened trunks, witness to the previous fire.

Fire plays an important role in Australian ecosystems, particularly in the Kwongan heath biosystem. The word 'Kwongan' is needless to say derived from a Noongar word where the meaning is not fully understood, however, it is used by botanists as a reference to the species rich low heaths that occur in south west. Even though the Kwongan heath covers no more than 25% of the south-west botanical region, it supports over 70% of the flora and of those species, over 50 % are endemic to Western Australia.

Wheatbelt farmers

Recently a Cunderdin farmer sadly died, still a relatively young man. His partner Wendy and children were of course totally devastated.

It was early summer and it was time to harvest. From far and wide farmers came with their big 4WD tractors and combined harvesters and mobile bins and storage trucks. In just a few days the crops were harvested, no money changed hands, it's just what you do to help those in need. I took a flight with a great pilot Sid, who flew low and high at speed, zooming in on the various tractors and machinery. The number of tractors in different paddocks was awesome and to witness the collective help made one feel proud to be Australian. Thanks to Sid, Nelson, Wendy and Gordon for helping make the flights happen — it was also great to see the help Wendy got and the camaraderie between the farming community.

Salt

Alas with land clearing for agriculture on a massive scale comes the down side of increased salination in surface soils.

What creates these salt laden lakes when once they had fresh or brackish water?. It's a complex process but in the past, particularly in the Wheatbelt Region, there were extensive woodlands that stretched right across the Wheatbelt. The trees drew the moistures from the soil in turn distributing excess into the atmosphere. Deep below the surface was subterranean ground water. When the trees were removed massive amounts of water seeped into the ground water. Over time the water levels rose entering dryer subsoils. These soils contain vast quantities of ancient salt crystals. As the water levels rose, these ancient salts dissolved in the rising waters eventually rising into the root levels of trees which in turn drew on the high salt laden waters into the root system, eventually killing the living trees particularly in the lower drainage areas. Where trees were totally cleared, the saline waters were drawn close to the surface. Over time, these exposed soils dried out fast and soils became less absorbent and when heavier rains fell the salt in the surface soils is washed into the low lying lakes, thus killing trees near the lakes and leaving salt deposits that line the water's edge and encrust poles or dead trunks in salt.

What is the answer to all of this? Well it's a massive problem and scientists, agriculturalists and farmers have been battling the problem in earnest since the 1970s. The damage is done and the work done to make drainage lines and plant trees has run not into millions but billions.

◀ **A small salt-ridden lake on the Quairading-Bruce Rock Road**

I could show you photographs of many sunny beaches with board flat seas, and cloudless blue skies with which Western Australia is certainly blessed with, however, inclement weather, stormy skies, amazing sunsets, dawn colours and after sunset light make for a far more dynamic and challenging photograph for me.

Many professional photographers now play with Photoshop and other software packages to alter colours, drop in boat jetties that aren't there or pump up colours to ridiculous levels. I feel every one should do what they feel comfortable doing, however I like to try and not alter the colours too much or the aspects of the land. I prefer the natural wild lights of nature to enhance my photographs, although if I do wish to impart a feeling such as creating, like a monochrome or increased shading in areas then I will adjust. There is of course a down side with producing true colours with the big presses that print books. They all use the simple four-colour process CMYK (cyan, magenta, yellow, and key-black). Unlike the RGB process in printing, that allows for a far greater colour range, the CMYK process really makes it difficult to replicate the original natural colours in a photograph. It tends to darken, alter reds and kills blues. To over come this one has to use a variety of adjustments particularly saturation to stop the photograph becoming dull and lifeless. It's certainly a challenge and rarely gives you a 100% colour correct look.

◀ **Lights Beach near Denmark**

Canola crop central Wheatbelt

What stories they could tell

Grasstrees near Spencers Brook

▶ Baladong Farm in York

Balladong Farm

Just across the road from my 1856 cottage in the town of York Western Australia are some of the original buildings of one of the first farms in WA, known as Balladong Farm. On this land back in 1831 Rivett Bland and Arthur Trimmer built some of the first buildings in York, setting up the first Government Stock Station.

Bland and Trimmer within only a year had developed a substantial sheep flock. Roe writes in his journal in November 1832, when doing further surveying of the York area. *"Here these gentlemen have located themselves with a flock of more than 500 sheep, mostly merino and other superior kinds and are doing very well"*. John Lort Stokes when visiting York a few years later in July 1838, wrote in his journal *"..I may mention that we found Mr Bland, the most wealthy colonist in Western Australia, engaged in holding the plough"* although he was a bit dismissive of the quality of land.

Bland was the first settler in the area to have a wool press as well as a basic mill and granary. On the 24th November 1834 he was appointed Resident Magistrate and later he established Balladong Farm in 1836. Bland's sheep were doing so well on the pastures of the Avon Valley, that Dr Harris in October, 1834, when addressing the Agricultural Society in Guildford said *"No country in the world can boast of grounds more favourable for sheep than the York district of this Colony, where some flocks have been for some time established with such success as to dispel every doubt and clear the prospects of the settlers at large"*. The Society realized that over the hills in the Avon valley the land was far more suited to grain growing and the Swan River more so for vegetables and fruit growing.

It was the Parker dynasty that was to develop Balladong Farm as well as Bridge House and Balladong House located nearby. The first Parker to settle in York was Stephen Henry Parker Snr from Lyminge Kent in England . He established the property Northbourne ten miles south of York. Both his sons Stephen Stanley and John Wyborn Parker developed other grants. Stephen improved Balladong and the farm buildings you can see in the photographs were developed by the Parkers. The Parker family became one of the leading early pioneer families in Western Australia. Other pioneering families like Marwick, Monger, Fleay, Duperouzel and Seabrook families still reside in the York area.

Balladong has recently been purchased by Mathew Reed, a progressive thinker, who will hopefully in time, restore this national heritage back to its former self. Alas, it's never a cheap process bringing the old back to life.

In the photograph I have reduced the colour saturation to give a feel of antiquity.

Mount Caroline

Mount Caroline is located about 30 kms north east of the town of Quairading. For those interested in early European history. In November 1830, the explorer Ensign Dale with three newly arrived settlers Clarkson, Hardey and Camfield made the furthest exploration inland from Perth that any European had ventured and it was Mount Stirling and Mount Caroline that they came to. Mount Caroline is named 'Mulyeen' or 'Moulein' by the local indigenous group the Balladong people.

This massive granite outcrop for the naturalist holds a special interest. It supports the largest population in the south-west of the vulnerable Black-flanked Rock-wallaby. There are several populations of this species scattered throughout WA and in central Australia. They are timid creatures and have been greatly affected by predation of the European fox and feral cat, so much so that they will not venture far from their cave retreats which limits the range of their foraging.

Luckily the few south-west populations have been brought back from the brink of extermination by the implementation of peripheral fences around the base of the granite rocks where they live. One rock population was down to five individuals with only one female, however with fencing and the introduction of some individuals from other rocks, the population went from 5 to over 100 a wonderful outcome for this endangered species.

The rock habitats selected by the species are large granite rocks that have enough cracks and caves where they can retreat to during the day, coming out to graze at dusk. In the winter, they can be seen warming themselves in the morning sun.

On Mount Caroline grow some rare plants like the restricted eucalypt, *Eucalyptus caesia* subsp. *caesia*. Many people who see this beautiful weeping mallee that is seen growing in Perth, with its bright pink flowers in May and June do not realize it is highly restricted in its distribution, occurring on only 8 or so granite rocks. For those who have an interest in eucalypts, there is an excellent book titled 'Eucalypts of Western Australia's Wheatbelt' No wonder the author Malcolm French chooses to live very close to Mount Caroline as there are restricted eucalypts growing nearhis property.

(Please note, the general public unfortunately cannot enter Mount Caroline as it is surrounded by private property, which is a good thing in a way as the rock wallaby is such a nervous little critter. However, close by one can visit Kokerbin Rock just north of the small town of Kwolyin.)

▶ **Looking towards Cliffy Head west of Walpole**

Albany 420 miles from Perth Looking from Torndirrup National Park one can see across King George Sound and Princess Royal Harbour towards the southern city of Albany.

Albany is a growing town, with much to offer for both the visitor and resident. It is steeped in history both indigenous and early European. It is the oldest European settled town in Western Australia being founded in 1826 as a military garrison and outpost for New South Wales. It has a far superior natural harbour than that in Fremantle, however with the blasting of the limestone bar at Fremantle and subsequent dredging, Fremantle became the lead port.

Recently Albany commemorated the 100 years since the First and Second Convoy of the ANZAC fleet first departed King George Sound to fight in 'The Great War'. On board the many vessels were over 40,000 Australian and New Zealand soldiers. There was also an estimated 17,000 horses. The illustrations shown on Anzac Hill show some of the 54 Australian and New Zealand ships anchored in King George Sound must have been an awesome sight even by today's standards.

Ocean Beach near Denmark

Goldfields & Desert

The Goldfields has a character all of its own. You can see it etched in its early history. When Arthur Bayley registered a claim at Fly Flat in Coolgardie in 1892, the 'Goldrush' had commenced. A year later when the Irishmen Patrick Hannan, Tom Flanagan and Daniel Shea were forced to camp due to one of their horses loosing a shoe at Mt Charlotte, it was to turn out to be the most fortunate mishap, for over the next two days they found over 100 ounces of alluvial gold. That cemented the 'Goldrush' and within a few years Coolgardie had 30,000 people living under tin and canvas. Today, there are still 6th generation miners working the huge open pit on the Golden Mile in Kalgoorlie. Our photographic journey here takes us from the stony Goldfields, way out to country that is very close to my heart, the desert regions. This is a vast area covering half of Western Australia. It can be uncompromising and if you are ill equipped to enter these remote areas it may be your demise. There were some amazing exploits across these vast spinifex clad sand dune deserts. The list is long, John and Alexander Forrest, Peter Warburton, David Carnegie, Ernest Giles, Frank Hann, Alfred Canning, Samuel Talbot, William Everard, Francis Gregory and many more. Many of these expeditions had the objective of finding inland waters or better pastoral country. What they did find were miles and miles of desert sand dunes and certainly no large bodies of permanent water. They often came close to death in their exploits. First, they used horses to explore and found these poor creatures totally inadequate for this form of travel and camels became by far the best solution. Some were kind to the indigenous inhabitants, some were certainly not. The one man that has made desert exploration far more accessible for 4WD vehicles was the amazing Len Beadell, surveyor, roadbuilder extraordinaire and amazing character, who himself came close to death in the deserts. He developed numerous tracks that traversed much of central Australia including the Anne Beadell Highway, The Connie Sue, The Gunbarrel, The Gary Highway and The Gary Junction Road. The photographs included here are often taken far from the nearest civilization and I hope they impart the joy that I get from being alone in some very special places.

The above photograph is looking across the playa lake of Lake Cowan near Norseman. The lake is a classic example of the flat playa lakes that are scattered throughout the arid zone. They are formed in what was once ancient valleys that we know as palaeodrainage systems which have long been filled with clays and silt and are heavily salt encrusted as the mineral salts can no longer reach the sea. These salt lakes are normally bone dry but are treacherous to cross when wet.

Western Woodlands Many years ago when I took bird tours through the Great Western Woodlands I would mention to people that I thought this was possibly the largest extensive uncleared woodland I know in Australia, I was reasonably qualified to say that then as I literally had been to most areas throughout Australia many, many times while running bird tours. I knew that from well north of Coolgardie and south to Esperance and then from west at the Vermin Fence way east of Balladonia lay this vast area of eucalypt woodland. Now it is a well known fact and great conservation work is now being done to recognize and protect the largest remaining Mediterranean climate woodland in the world.

The quantity of species of eucalypt in this region is staggering. Luckily due to the region being relatively dry with low rainfall, clearing for farming past the Vermin Fence did not occur. Some trial blocks were tried but the agricultural board recommended that it was too arid for farming, so we are left with this vast area of woodland. There are mines in the region but for now, the land remains in a relative pristine state. Well over 200 species of eucalypt lie within the confines of this region. I was talking to someone who had received a grant to continue a major research project in the woodlands. I asked who was assisting with the funds as it was privately funded. I found the answer interesting. A large percentage of the donations came from eastern states private citizens. Why? Well, it was concluded from the discussion that they felt so much of the semi-arid woodland both in south-eastern Queensland and particularly NSW had been drastically cleared and they wanted this large area of uncleared woodland to survive. How our priorities shift particularly in later life, as to what is important before we depart this little planet of ours.

Lake Ballard

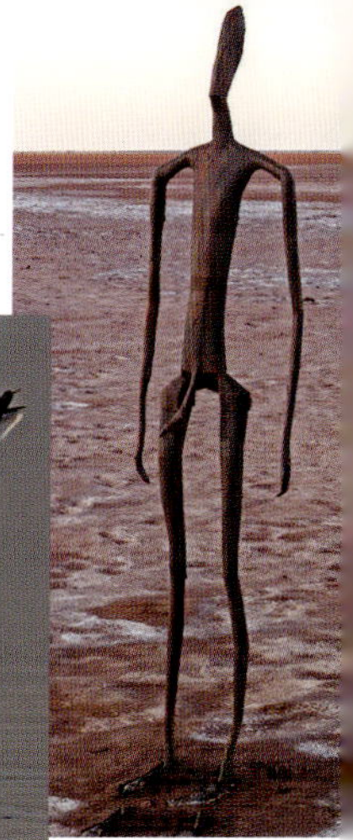

Lake Ballard lies approximately 130 kms north of Kalgoorlie in the Goldfields.

The Shire of Menzies and other government agencies are to be commended for allowing the British sculptor Antony Gormley a free hand in producing these 51 life size sculptures. We need the artists of this world to show that the left-side-brained world of money and status is not everything. Antony's sculptures were meant to be a temporary installation titled 'Inside Australia' being part of the Perth International Arts Festival. Well luckily the Turner Prize winners works had such an impact, that they were left intact on this distant salt lake.

On a side note, there are information boards at Lake Ballard about Banded Stilt. For many, birds are not a big deal but this particular species is perhaps more intriguing than many. Ornithologists saw this bird regularly on the odd salt lakes scattered throughout the south-west, particularly the salt lakes on Rottnest Island where the early European settlers nicknamed them 'Rottnest Snipe'. The birds were recorded in the late 1800's but the question for many, was where did these birds breed. It was not until as late as the early 1930s that they were discovered breeding in their thousands on Lake Grace in the eastern wheatbelt. Banded Stilt are highly nomadic, that is, they will travel anywhere in the Australia, normally in remote regions, where there have been extensive rains. The inland playa lakes when inundated, form small islands on the higher ground within the lake system. It's here where the safety of surrounding waters stop predations from foraging animals.

These colonies can have staggering numbers with over 150,000 birds breeding in one area. If the lakes dry out too fast, then the mortality rate is extremely high but generally the high breeding numbers allow the early hatched birds to survive. These shallow lakes dry out fast and one year the residents of the town of Menzies some 50 kms away from Lake Ballard had birds too young to fly, literally walking down the high street. It must have been a sad sight for many who would have felt helpless to assist.

Peak Charles Known by the Ngadju people as Karrukarrunya, Peak Charles thrusts itself up from the relatively flat plain around it. It is a huge solid mass of granite magma that has more feldspar and less quartz than is found in most granites. This huge mass of magna would have forced its way through faults in the Yilgarn Craton forming this dome shaped mountain.

It has several rare plants that occupy the higher slopes of the mountain, one is on the left of the picture the *tuberous calothamnus*.

Helena Aurora Range This is one of the few remaining high BIF (Banded Ironstone Formation) ranges north of Koolyanobbing not being mined. I certainly am not totally against mining as I'm a realist and the world asks for minerals and we dig them up and employment occurs. However, some areas are quite spectacular and in a relatively pristine state. My argument not to mine this unique and beautiful range is that within this northern Yilgarn region, most of the ranges have or are being mined such as Windarling, Mt Jackson and of course Koolyanobbing. For me it's a case of when is enough, enough. The mining game goes up and down like a yoyo and mines close and open and I certainly feel for anyone who loses jobs or needs one and I know guys who are losing jobs but in the long term if we take out the last magnificent banded ironstone range, what's left for the future. I'm not even mentioning 'save the rare plants' even though I know there are two rare and restricted plants on the top of the range. No, it's as I say, when is enough, enough. Mine somewhere else but leave this magnificent range alone. For those who have not seen it, take your 4WD out and see it but be careful, there are mining tracks all over the place but when you get to the top of the Helena Aurora park the car and look at the magnificent vista.

It was a very warm day as I drove down the Mulga Park track south of the Great Central Road. I decided to take a siesta and parked the vehicle under a huge sheoak tree, the same species as the tree set against the setting sun on the left. In my half sleep, I could hear the constant begging call of a juvenile parrot, typical of young when wanting parents to regurgitate food. I thought it must be a Corella a common parrot, so I lay there not bothering but the call did not sound right, so up I got and stepped outside to investigate. There on the branch over hanging my vehicle were 3 beautiful Pink Cockatoo's (also known as Major Mitchell's Cockatoo) illustrated above. These stunning looking parrots are often found in the desert regions where the desert sheoaks grow.

These are some of the most southerly Desert Sheoaks to be found in Western Australia.

▶ **Marble Gums on the Great Central Road**

Mt Warsop

Looking west from Mt Warsop, I'm standing where John Forrest stood on the 15th July 1874 and 23 years later David Carnegie and his offsider Charles Stansmore.

The photograph is certainly not an award winning shot, but it's included here as the area is very remote and not far from the Mt Warsop, is a small soak known as Alexander Springs. When one hears the word 'springs' it conjures in the mind fresh water oozing up to the surface but alas, this is not the case here and even current maps write the words 'permanent springs' (which would be solid gold out here in the Victoria Desert) Alas, it's a simple soak. When I was here 20 plus years ago it held water, in 2015 there was none as it was generally a dry year before.

The first European to find the soak was Alexander Forrest with the indigenous tracker Tommy Pierre. Alexander was accompanying his brother John Forrest who was leading his third major expedition into unknown lands. John named this life saving soak after his brother.

The objective of the Forrest brothers' expedition was to see if there was an inland lake system. Well, there were no large freshwater lagoons but they did traverse a vast area, travelling from Geraldton to Adelaide. Several times on this expedition they came close to death and had to put down several of the horses.

In 1897, another extraordinary explorer David Carnegie and his party visited Alexander Springs. They were luckier finding water in Woodhouse Lagoon not far away, however they had nearly died days before when luckily, after much pressuring of an indigenous old man, they were led to Empress Springs.

As I left the Great Central Road heading for Alexander Springs I passed no whites or blacks on the track over the 160 km journey but just as I was getting close to my destination, there was an indigenous family group in the middle of the track waving me down. Their broken down vehicle was a kilometre away on Woodhouse Lagoon, which was bone dry. I took one guy on the bonnet with feet stretched onto the bull bars, as I had removed the passenger seat. We found them after bush bashing over samphire and sand. I pumped up the punctured tyre with the electric pump and gave them plugs, then cranked up their dead battery and they staggered out of the lagoon towing their trailer. When we got back to the main group of about 3 adults and four or five children, I gave away some of my 'gold' – 20 litres of water.

I mention this story not because I'm some kind of hero, no, I mention it because there is sadly, a disconnect with the land in terms of practical knowledge being passed on down as well as survival techniques. Much knowledge is going fast and this is really, really sad as this is remote country and uncompromising (I need to emphasis that the disconnect does not apply to all desert indigenous people I know).

The main problem is the use of old run down vehicles, while running they will cover great distances. The 4WD vehicle I use cost huge bucks and the quantity of gear we carry to protect ourselves from satellite phones to complex recovery gear is also highly costly. Alas, many indigenous people cannot afford these high costs. On the plus side indigenous people are far more relaxed about life and their mortality compared with Europeans, I should know, I've travelled with whites who are so uptight with the fear and potential loss of their precious life that takes all the joy out of remote travel.

The down side for indigenous folk is that in the past before Europeans came, they walked everywhere and knew the land like the back of their hand, particularly where all the water holes were and they were always within walking distance. You take a car 280 kms away from your home and it breaks down, you will not walk back that distance with insufficient water.

I returned back to the community and luckily they all got back home after families drove out to get them.

▶ **The Blackstone Range east of Warburton**

The sun has set at Giles Breakaway on the Great Central Road

◀ *Previous page* On Mt Fanny looking east as the sun rises over the Mulga Park Road, Victoria Desert

It started to rain that night at Giles Breakaway – time to get out of the desert regions

▶ Sun setting over the Spinifex Great Central Road

Mid-West

Stretching from roughly Lancelin all the way north to Carnarvon and across to the western edge of our deserts, is a land of millions of hectares of mulga woodland and rocky outcrops supporting many sheep stations. It is here in the Mulga, if reasonable winter rains have fallen there can be the most spectacular displays of everlastings that cover the hillsides. Over these pages I show some of the spectacular displays that await the traveller.

In this region there are also miles and miles of sandy beaches, particularly in the Shark Bay area where many travellers come to see the inquisitive dolphins that visit Monkey Mia near Denham.

Kalbarri is relatively close to Perth and there is always something flowering in Kalbarri National Park even in summer when the Banksia displays can be spectacular, although late August to early November is the high point. The Murchison winds its way through the sandstone gorges cutting its way to the estuary at Kalbarri.

Everlastings in the old holding paddock, Gabyon Station

Everlastings in the Mulga

The Mulga region covers a huge tract of land from the northern wheatbelt up to the Pilbara region in the north-west and across to central Australia. It's a land that receives little rainfall but in good seasons the land is transformed into a blaze of colour. When travelling through the country, the dry red soils are bare and denuded but under that crust of sun-baked soil lies the seeds of the daisy family, the genus 'Asteraceae', the second largest family group in Australia. When good rains fall, the seeds germinate and the resultant displays of colour are unbelievable. If you drive say from Paynes Find to Yalgoo (dirt road) in a good season, the changing colours of the differing species of everlasting will amaze. It's important to check where most rains have fallen in the drier regions of the State. If the Pilbara area has had good rains then the Tall Mulla Mulla will cover lots of the mulga lands as well as the Featherheads. Sometimes the coastal belt, particularly around Overlander Roadhouse where the turn off to Shark Bay is, can have spectacular displays of everlastings if rains have been more coastal. If the inland road from Wubin all the way to Mt Newman has had good rains, then this route will have less tourist traffic and the reward is that the colours of the everlastings will keep changing as you head north. If the Goldfields and southern desert regions have had exceptional rains, the Central Road to Warburton and Giles can have diverse displays of everlastings with differing colours.

Reynoldson Reserve

After the sun has set, the Pink Morrison (*Verticordia monadelpha*) glows in the after light in Reynolds Reserve just north of Wongan Hills. The name 'monadelpha' has its origins in the Greek words 'monos' meaning 'solitary' and 'adelphos' meaning 'brother'. Well, it's certainly a case of 'brothers in arms' here as these beautiful flowers mass together.

This small reserve preserves some of the last remaining local concentrations of the feather flowers (Verticordias) to be seen in this region. Even though the reserve is only about 10 acres or so, it contains six species of feather flowers. Here in the picture, the Pink Morrison dominates with small clumps of the white Common Cauliflower verticordia (*V. eriocephala*) scattered throughout. If you are lucky, you may see the rare Wongan Featherflower (*V. wonganensus*) if you visit the reserve in late spring.

The land was originally owned by William. H. Reynoldson who decided to set aside this flora rich area. Alas just before the land was excised, William died and the next owner, Percy Conway had no idea it was going to be set aside and unfortunately started to plough up the land. Luckily another local farmer stopped Percy, who mentioned the situation to him. To his credit, Percy decided to set aside double the area and so today the precious little reserve gives pleasure to so many flower lovers.

To see the bright feather flower displays, the verticordia's you have to come in late spring (November).

Verticordias are almost exclusively a Western Australian genus with over 100 species and only a few species in the Northern Territory. They are commonly known as the 'feather flowers' due to the feathered appearance of the flower fringes. One of the favourite flora books in my library is the book 'Verticordia' by Elizabeth (Berndt) George and illustrated by the wonderful nature artist Margaret Pieroni. The subtitle is called 'The turner of hearts' which was derived from the Latin 'vertocor'. They are a truly beautiful genus and when seen in mass are a sight to behold.

Coalseam Reserve south-east of Geraldton is the most reliable area to see everlasting most years

Everlastings south of Cue There is a lot of misinformation regarding the flowering times for everlastings. If there have been no decent rains in the summer or early winter, then few if any everlastings will bloom. If people arrive in WA in say, late October or November with the hope of seeing everlastings. Most will have dried up and scattered across the dry mulga plains. Yes they are called 'everlastings' but in the wild they will be in bloom for only a few weeks. The yellow everlastings are the yellow Pompom Heads The pink dwarf bush scattered amongst the everlastings, is the Cotton Bush.

In the mulga region of the mid-west, the early pastoral stations were opened up for sheep grazing as early as the 1850s and there was no wire available for fencing so these early holding yards, like the one shown above, were fenced using the local mulga.

The first Europeans to open up the country for sheep grazing, went over the Darling Range and settled in York in 1831 but within the first 20 years they had expanded their flocks to such numbers in the Avon Valley that several of the successful farmers moved stock north, first to the Champion Bay region and then later they spread to the mulga woodland east of Mullewa and north to the Murchison and on to the Pilbara.

▶ **The Pinnacles near Cervantes**

The Pinnacles These tombstone-like pillars protrude up from the bright yellow sands near the small township of Cervantes. The geological process that created these limestone rich columns, evolved from the process of rains leaching through the harder calcrete layers way back in the Pleistocene times. It's a very complex process and I wont attempt to go through the detailed chemistry that brought about the harder limestone rich columns that remained after winds in dryer times blew away the softer, less compacted sands. It is so complex, that geologists still debate the whole evolutionary process, however, if you ever visit the area, the information centre in the park details the suggested formation of how these columns evolved over time.

The following three photographs were taken within a two hour period and show how light changes rapidly, to create differing moods that you see here.

Wooleen

Wooleen Station near the Murchison River north of Mullewa.

The rich red-ochre rocks glow with the setting sun on Wooleen Station, a memorable place to visit. Wooleen is a particularly impressive station having a diverse range of habitat types from huge granite outcrops to a large lake system. It is run by a lovely young couple David and Francis Pollock. They run an alternative cattle station where by limiting stock numbers, where they try not to overgraze areas However, they still have to try and survive financially which is no easy task.

Kalbarri   The sun has just set at Ross Graham lookout in Kalbarri National Park.

The Murchison River cuts its way through the relatively soft Tumblagooda Sandstone. People who are interested in fossils often come to the park to see the ancient marine life that is embedded in these ancient sea-beds. This is almost the most northerly region where high numbers of differing wildflowers can be seen in mass and for the enthusiast, starting in Kalbarri say in late August and then slowly working one's way south till late November the traveller can see the best range of wildflowers the state has to offer, although Kalbarri will always have reasonable displays of flowers all through this period.

Hamelin Bay   Here in these shallow waters at the southern part of Shark Bay grow one of the planet's oldest life forms. The waters in Hamelin Bay are twice as salty as the open seas and yet even in the searing heat of summer and the tidal exposure to the sun, primitive minute bacteria known as cyanobacteria fuse together to make what's known as Microbial Mats. Over time the mats trap sand and form flat structures but in deeper water they can form columns and biologists call them Stromatolites (picture alongside). It's under the microscope that their amazing world can be seen.

Monkey Mia I think Monkey Mia has good value for the visitor in terms of location, attractions and accommodation. Yes, the Dolphins are the main reason people come here. To see the interaction of these intelligent creatures with the rangers who occasionally feed them is a real buzz for a first timer. For me viewing the placid waters that stay calm throughout most of the year including winter is the main joy, particularly at sunset.

▶ **Stormy skies south of Eagle Bluff. Shark Bay**

Pilbarra

The Pilbara Region covers a diverse range of habitats but at its core is the vast Archaean Pilbara Craton, a massive area of some of the oldest bedrock granites in the world. It's a geologist dream and a miner's delight and they are certainly busy there. I first visited the mine at Tom Price in the late 1970s and the mine site is still going all these years later, although much has changed with many new mining sites opening up since I first came.

Karijini National Park is luckily unspoilt and a great place to see the magnificent geology and colours of the central Pilbara. The white trunk snappy gums that dot the landscape are a photographer's delight set against the rust-red rocks. When one ventures into the deep gorges, the colours of the Banded Ironstone are something else, best seen in Hamersley Gorge and Weano Gorge area particularly in the gorge where Kermit's Pool is located. I wanted to get an even better shot this year with my 62 mp camera but alas the water was far too high to wade through and it was certainly not worth losing a very expensive camera so other gorges took Kermit's place.

The highest mountain in Western Australia lies in the Hamersley Range, namely Mount Meharry named after the Chief Geodetic Surveyor in the 1950s. It peaks at 1249 m, low in world terms but high for WA. The true height was established in 1967. Some 80 kms away is the second highest mountain and that is Mt Bruce being only 15 m lower. No wonder the Karijini in mid July can be cold as the general altitude within the park is at least 1000 m.

I have walked in many of the gorges in the lower ranges and there are many rock etchings that the Kurrama, Banyjima and Yinhawangka people have carved their dreaming stories in the red rocks. The information centre in Karijini has a lot of interesting information on indigenous history. Many people think that the rock etchings known as petroglyphs are restricted to the Burrup Peninsula area but they are spread right across the Pilbara to the edge of the Western Deserts, although I agree that if you wish to see these engravings in profusion then the Burrup certainly has by far the greatest concentrations of these interesting rock art etchings.

▶ **Kalamina Gorge, Karijini**

Karijini The geology and evolution of the rock types in Karijini is certainly fascinating to me. It's hard to imagine that the rocks you see in Karijini started their origins as small grains of sediment which over time built up on the ancient seabeds 2500 mya. There was less Oxygen then and the only life was very primitive bacteria. The sediments were rich in silica and iron. The sediments piled up and up and with the continued pressure they turned into hardened rock. When the continents collided, these tectonic plates created massive horizontal pressures when they collided and created the folds you can see on page 120 and 131 in Hamersley Gorge. The alternating coloured bands consist of iron-poor sediments and iron-rich sediments. With the continued pressure faults in the uplifted bed-rocks occurred and then over time weathering of flowing water creating the gorges you see today.

The iron rich BIF (Banded Ironstone Formation) is found throughout the Hamersley Range and millions of tons are exported every year.

On a humorous note, the small picture alongside shows a pile of small pebbles. This is not the work of some energetic road worker shovelling stones but the work of a very industrious little critter, *Pseudomys chapmani* more commonly known as the Western Pebble Mound Mouse, weighing in at just 12 – 15 grams. This little rodent picks up small pebbles with its fore paws and puts them in their mouth and carries them to where the burrow is. They slowly pile the pebbles completely covering the burrow. The mountain you see behind the mound is a famous hill. It's called 'The Governor', named by the early explorer Ernest Giles, and has high concentrations of iron ore. Well, a large mining company spent a lot of money drilling and testing but they forgot to do a thorough environmental impact study. Well they missed this uncommon and restricted little critter in their project. Back in Perth in the head office a senior executive, lets just call him 'John'. While he was walking through the general office area a fellow manger said 'You don't look very happy John, what's the matter', his answer, 'They found a f...... mouse'! If you take the Newman – Port Hedland road you will pass this impressive mountain adjacent to a 24 hour overnight stop, yes it's still standing, and the little critters keeps doing their thing.

Over the next few pages I show the beautiful diversity of this mountain range park Karijini with its many gorges, stepped waterfalls and cool pools. For the traveller though, be very careful as there have been many deaths in these deep gorges, mainly caused from falling off rock ledges also flash floods have been another cause. The saddest death for me was the gallant State Emergency Rescuer James 'Jim' Regan who tragically got caught in a flash flood only minutes after he had just finished tying up the rescue ropes to save a stranded UK lass in Hancock Gorge. If you do visit Karijini, you will love the park but do be careful. I return to this text a week or so later, reason, yet another fatality in Karijini, another tourist has died falling from a rock ledge, I'll say no more on this.

Fortescue Falls in Dale Gorge. Karijini

▶ Over the page, the multi coloured Hamersley Gorge. Then all next three pages in Dale Gorge.

119

Fern rock wall in Dale Gorge

◀ *Previous page* **Kalimina Gorge**

The multi-coloured rock strata in Hamersley Gorge

Leaving Karijini as the sunsets

▶ High in the Hamersley Range

Previous page ◀ **Sunrise on Mt Herbert**

Python Pool lies below Mt Herbert on the little used Roebourne-Wittenoom Road

▶ Weano Gorge, Karijini

After sunset

I'm camped high in the Hamersley Range. I took a shot of the sun setting in the valley below my camping rig. A good 20 minutes after the sun had set I looked at the beautiful white snappy gums on the moonlight night. I found the feeling of the photograph far more evocative than the setting sun shot I took earlier. The larger mega-pixel cameras have an amazing capacity to capture light well after the sun has set.

▶ **Looking up to the mountains of the Hamersley Range off the Munjina Road**

◀ Over 100 million tons of iron ore each year leave the Hamersley Range destined for the various parts of the world. I find young people use the phrase 'it's awesome' for anything, even if they are just chewing on a hamburger. Well for me the size of the mining infrastructure in Port Headland is certainly awesome. How homo sapiens, like little ants can collectively create such huge facilities and vast rail systems is remarkable.

▶ I have just driven my 4WD weighing over one ton up one of the stoniest and steepest tracks in Western Australia climbing up Mt Nameless, adjacent to Tom Price. I had to laugh when I read some notes after I made the drive. 'The track is a gravel road' well they were the largest pieces of gravel I've seen, some boulders being 200 mm in diameter. It was until recently the highest mountain one could drive up. There is a spectacular 360 degree view at the top showing the magnificence of this part of the Hamersley Range.

The red-ochre rocks glow in the setting sun just 20 kms east of Nanutarra Road House.

The Ashburton River is one of the most southerly of the big rivers that drain from the Pilbara region to the Indian Ocean. The other big rivers are the Fortescue. Sherlock, Yule, Robe, De Grey and Turner. All of them, when the Pilbara receives cyclonic rains have massive volumes of water flowing down them and are only surpassed by the mighty Fitzroy River when in flood.

The Kimberley

I'm often asked if I prefer the Kimberley or the Pilbara. Well the gorges in the Hamersley Range are beautiful and colours so varied but a love of a region can develop not through the vision of the scenery alone but also what the country brings to your inner self. For me, it's about getting away from the masses, finding solitude in places where it is peaceful and if the scenery is beautiful as well, then that is an added bonus.

Over the pages there will be photographs that exemplify that feeling.

Our journey in the Kimberley will start in Broome, a town I well remember as a sleepy northern beach town with a casual multicultural feel about it. It still has that but four times the volume of people now. People say they are going to Broome up in the Kimberley but for me it's still not the Kimberley. Broome is surrounded by relatively flat country known as pindan woodland. It is Acacia woodland that stretches for many miles. The beaches are of course second to none here and if you drive up the Dampier Peninsula you can head off both east and west to beautiful quiet beaches.

The Kimberley for me really starts when I pass through Yammera Gap in the rugged limestone Napier Range near Windjana Gorge. The Gibb River road winds its way slowly higher and higher through the King Leopold Ranges. Our photographic journey will take us to Bell Gorge, Mornington Station, Mt Elizabeth Station then back to the Gibb River Road to Kununurra. Then to Wyndham and then south to Purnululu National Park before skirting around the southern border of the Kimberley back to Broome.

◀ Above Bell Gorge falls
▶ The multi coloured sandstone rocks on Roebuck Bay south of Broome

Cable Beach This is one beach that has certainly changed over the years. Once I would swim here among no more than 50 or 60 people, well look at the photo with the various marquees. There would be over a thousand people gathered here today and what is the event, a Polo match, something you would not dream of at Cable Beach years back. Most of the people playing Polo would be local Kimberley folk as this is horse country and some would drive hundreds of miles just to play. The various rodeos in the Kimberley also bring station people together and finer people you could not wish to meet.

The hard quartz rock that has survived the millions of floods that have passed through this narrow gorge at Windjana, has always to me had a Zen feel about it and I have adjusted the shading to impart that mystical feeling, so not your normal tourist picture here. The rock has greater meaning maybe to the traditional owners the Bunuba people who cal it Bandigan Rock.

Looking back at Yammera Gap in the Napier Range as the rising sun hits the sharp limestone ridge

▲▶ The stunning Bell Gorge at Silent Grove off the Gibb River Road

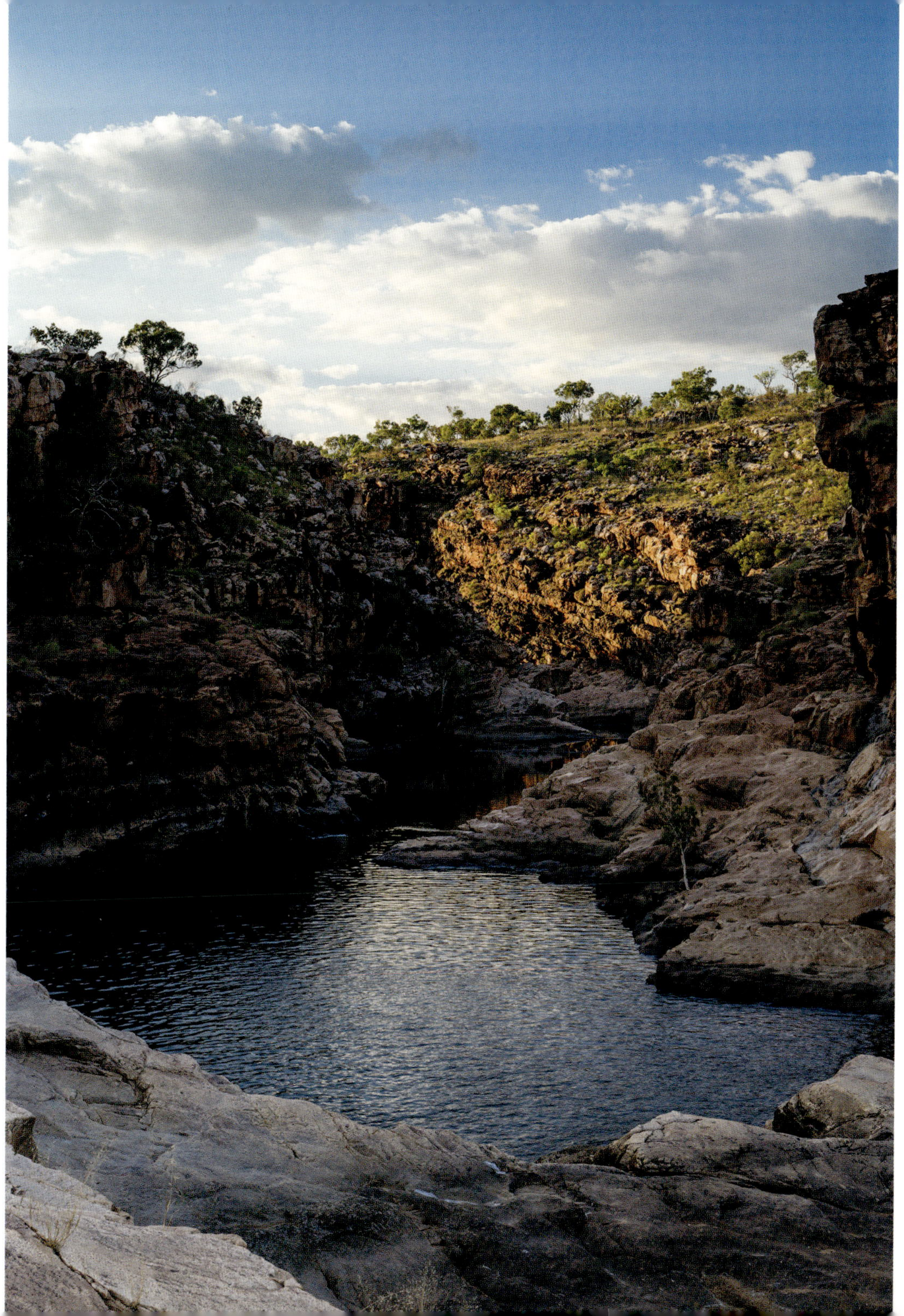

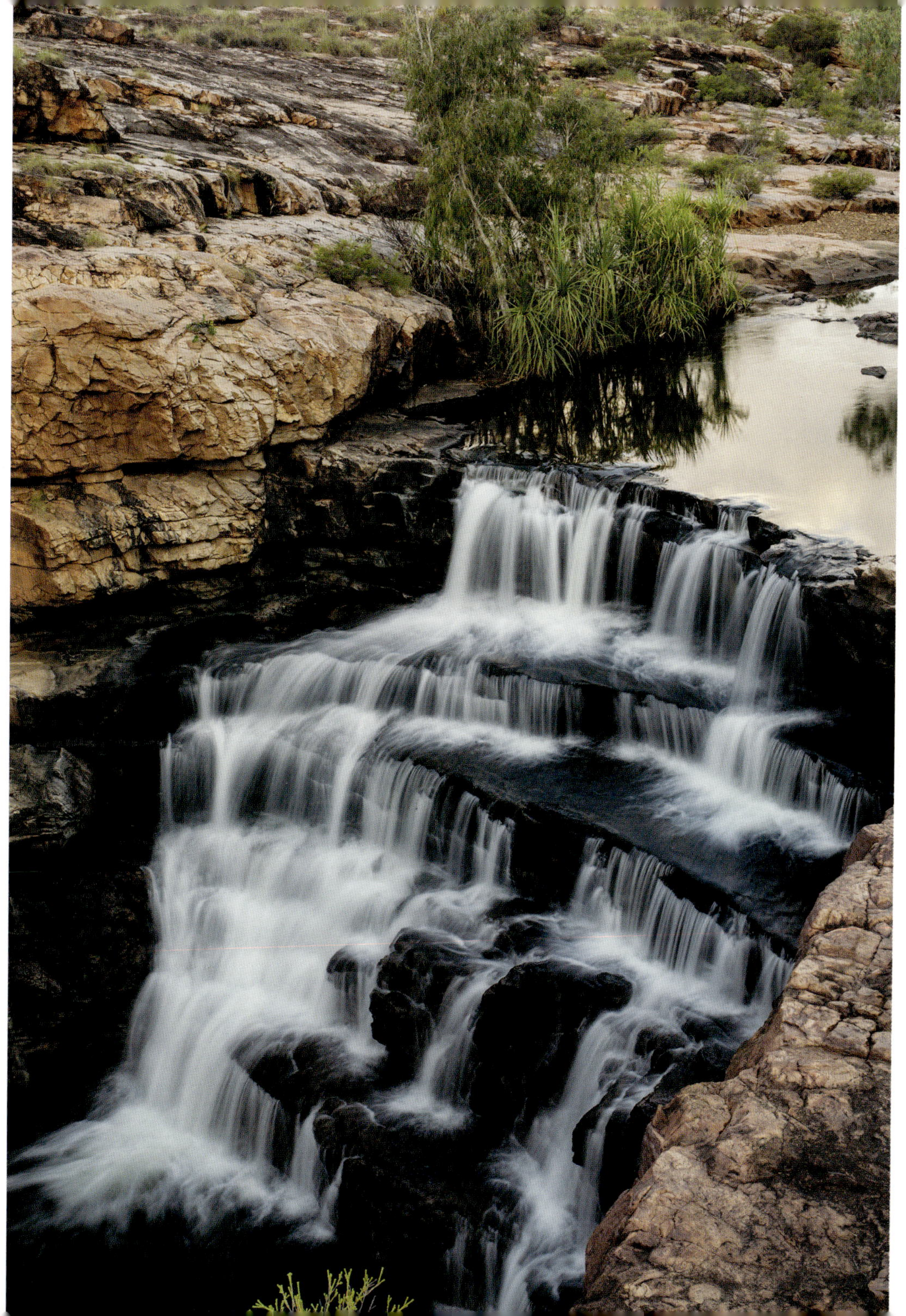

Mornington & Marion Downs Sanctuary

This large area of open tropical savannah and rugged hills and beautiful gorges, is run by the largest privately funded conservation landholder in Australia, the Australian Wildlife Conservancy (AWC) who manage over 7 million acres, that's a huge hunk of land. Knowing that conservation and environmental programs are being funded less and less by governments, either because they are seen as not being vote grabbing or simply of low priority in their budgetary programs makes me sad and I think it may be the private world that may come to the rescue of saving much of our fauna and wilderness areas.

While we are young having to raise families and establish homes, finding excess funds to support conservation programs can be difficult at times but many who are retired and have the time to reflect on where our little planet is heading, get very concerned and they do vote and many vote with their wallet funding organizations where they see real conservation work being done. These organizations have active monitoring programs that are helping us learn so much more about our rare fauna and flora and the most important thing is AWC is buying land that otherwise might have slowly become degraded by over use of livestock. We need to eat and we need produce but to keep some major parts of our country under the umbrella of a well organized conservation group can only assist the planet.

We hear so often that this species or that has now become exstinct or at least threatened and it becomes depressing. Well the AWC conducts regular site monitoring at Mornington and as an example the quantity of reptiles at Mornington has increased over the last 7 years and that shows that the understorey is healthier than in previous years.

Mammals are a major animal group that is declining at an alarming rate in Australia but at Mornington numbers seem to be stable and to have a species list of 38 mammal types in one region is relatively high compared with other semi-arid areas. If you want to have time out and see programs in action, you can stay in the wilderness camps at Mornington and see real conservation work taking place.

Two very uncommon species of birds are often mentioned at Mornington, the Purple-crowned Fairy-wren and the Gouldian Finch. I included a few of my shots taken in the wild for your interest. The Gouldian Finch is a stunning multi-coloured finch. Being primarily a seed-eater, it requires the seed of native grasses and with the various fire regimes in the Kimberley, there has been a great decline. I was talking to a station owner who has been on the land in the Kimberley for over 60 years and he told me that the Gouldian Finch was far more common when he was a young man.

You will notice both the black headed form and a red-headed form are shown, the rarest morph is a yellow-headed form.

The other species shown is a Purple-crowned Fairy-wren that lives in the thick sharp-edged pandanus palms that line the edge of slower running streams and pools.

▶ Sir John Gorge

Gibb River Road

The Gibb River road winds its way through the central Kimberley. It was once a rougher track to drive on but now it is relatively easy and each year more substantial work is done to upgrade the surface. It's not a really rugged 4WD track, you can almost do it in a normal 2WD now. Many hurtle along the Gibb River Road only venturing short distances say to Manning Gorge or Galvin's Gorge but to really get a true sense of the beauty of the Kimberley, it is best to stay on many of the stations that abut the Gibb River and Kalumburu Roads, there are fees obviously but the rewards far outweigh the small charges that are normally asked.

◀ **Galvins Gorge on the Gibb River Road**

▶ **Boabs well after sunset**

I had a whirlwind run this year to the Pilbara and Kimberley just to finish the shots for this book, doing over 10,000 kms in just 21 days, no way to travel but I'm getting my life back to where it was a few years back. I chose one location where I knew I could really relax and absorb the connection I have with this remote country. It was again, at the back of Peter and Pat Lacy's property about 60 plus kms along the Munja Track that is faithfully kept open by Rick and Ann Jane each year that takes you to their beautiful accommodated camp at Bachstein Gorge.

I wanted to slow down and that I did for two days alongside the pools of the upper Drysdale River. I walked into the hills close by and climbed high up on to the stony ridge tops looking across the vast wilderness knowing the nearest people were 50 kms away.

The following day I returned to an area I knew where to look for more Wandjina paintings, that remind me of a time long gone. This truly is a special place and I'm so privileged to be here. It's the ancestral land of the Ngoro Ngoro clan who are part of the larger group, the Ngarinyin people. Many Australians have little knowledge of the complex structure and the quantity of clan groups that exist the Kimberley. On the Munja Track alone, you pass through the clan groups of Ngoro Ngoro, Warrgalingongo, Galarungarri, Yunduma and that is just in a 150 km journey.

I had a hard walk getting to the top of this rugged range due to the two steel pins in my hip thanks to falling off my racing bike at speed - silly boy, but the pins are coming out hopefully.

Knowing I had this area just to myself with only the Friarbirds and the silver backed form of the Grey Butcherbird chuckling in the background – I was certainly connected and it was worth the 10,000 km run just to be here.

Not too far from this hill top one can find Wandjina paintings. The galleries are not as large as some of those found further west but they are still wonderful to find but also a sad reminder of way of life now gone since we came to these shores and certainly changed it for the first Australians.

The Wandjina paintings are the spirit figures that represent the creation or 'dreaming time'. David Mowaljarlai an indigenous elder described it as follows: "Wandjina came from the wind and travelled the land and made the earth and seas, and the mountains, the rivers, the waterholes, the trees, the plants, the animals, the language and then the people. Wandjina's made everything. Wandjina gave us the law to follow and gave us the land".

The serpent spirit above is similar to the Wagyl for the Noongars of the south-west. Rainbow serpents are important in creating pathways through the land and in the Kimberley the serpent has similar meanings and the elders would communicate with the dreamtime figures.

I wanted to photograph a special part of the Blackstone Range in central Australia but I was told I could not as it fell in the path of the dreamtime spirit that ran through the range all the way to Wiluna and I had to respect that even though the gorge and ridge would have made a wonderful photograph.

▶ **Bachstein Gorge off the Calder River**

The red afterglow near Lake Argyle

◀ After sunset leaving Lake Argyle

Lake Argyle

Named after the old cattle station that eventually was covered by the rising water that filled Lake Argyle.

There are some interesting facts regarding this artificial lake. It was completed in 1971 and contains 18 times the volume of water that Sydney Harbour has. It covers an area of 980 sq kms and initially was designed to irrigate 150,000 sq kms of farmland, but the initial project to develop rice fields was soon terminated when Magpie Geese ate the rice shoots faster than they could plant them. This was a common problem with all rice growing projects in the north such as at Fogg Dam near Darwin.

The dam wall in the photograph is 335 m long and the wall height 98 m. It is interesting that the spill-way wall was raised just 6 m in 1996 and it doubled the dam's capacity.

▶ **Boabs off the Kununurra – Wyndam Road**

Road into Purnululu (Bungle Bungle)

In the late 1980s it took me at least 3 to 4 hours to drive the 53 km track into Purnululu such was the ruggedness of the track. I remember taking bird watchers into the park in the converted 12 seater Land Cruiser where I had all the passengers out of the car and as many as possible stood on the outside step boards leaning out to balance weight past the centre of gravity of the vehicle at one particular part of the track. As the years have gone by the track has been improved and even off road camper trailers can get in but still not caravans, they must be based at the start of the track just off the highway. I find this country close to the entry of the park some of the most beautiful spinifex clad hills one can drive through.

Purnululu

Purnululu was vested as a World Heritage area in 2003 and I think it deserves that honour. The unique domes with their multicoloured bands of the Devonian quartz sandstone are apparently one of the best examples of Karst sandstone tower geology in the world.

The whole of the area was once a massive uplifted mesa and over time faults were created in the sandstone and over millions of years water running through the cracks created the domes as the water cut its way to the lower ground.

The surface of the domes is very fragile consisting of layers of iron oxide and dark bands of what is known as a cyanobacterial crust, the surface of the dark bands actually have life-forms adhering to the surface and are single cell photosynthetic organisms.

The park is well laid out with two major walking areas both at the southern and northern end of the park. As stated in my previous panorama book, I have taken many chopper flights in my time but the Bungle Bungle flight is a must for those who want to really appreciate the geology of this area.

▶ Near Cathedral Gorge. Purululu

Near Cathedral Gorge. Purululu

China Wall Close to the town of Halls Creek is a 6 m tall solid quartz vein that thrust vertically from the surrounding spinifex hills. It is exposed at differing locations over its 20 km long range and is one of the longest quartz veins known and if you take a chopper from Halls Creek to the Bungles, you can see it in several localities.

The limestone ramparts of the long Devonian Reef encircle the Kimberley, from east of Derby all the way around to south of Wyndham. The limestone reef juts out in several locations, best seen from Windjana Gorge to Geikie Gorge area.

Water over time has washed the softer coral sands leaving a very jagged surface on the exposed reef. This reef was not formed from ancient corals but older life forms in the way of algae and lime secreting organisms that are now long extinct.

The Bunuba people call *Geikie Gorge Darngku*.

Acknowledgements

I wish to thank Diane Beckingham for doing the first editing of text as 'The first reader' also for your advice and support throughout the final stages of this publication.

To HeliSpirit in the Kimberley for helping with this project. HeliSpirit fly throughout the Kimberley and run a very good professional operation.

To Leanne Quince of Graphics Above. This is our fourteenth year I think working together on another book and over the years we have never had an angry word between us, even if at times the pressure and deadlines were sometimes stressful – I truly thank you for that Leanne.

To the many Department of Parks and Wildlife staff I know who work under a really restricted and decreasing budgets, I thank you simply for doing what you do so well.

To Davy Yu for being so efficient with my printing work, always coming back fast with the answers I require, your company is lucky to have you Davy.

Over the last few years I have retreated into my work and neglected many, many good friends but unfortunately it's a case of 'catch up' on my life but those I do see, I simply thank you for being there.

Dedication

I dedicated my first photographic panorama book to Willy Teo over four years ago and I still dedicate my new panorama book to him. Willy has seen me through four difficult years since my last book.

It's rare in this world that one finds a person who was born on the opposite side of the globe but holds the same principles and moral code that I'd like to think I have. I thank you for being patient with my inadequate right-sided brain when it comes to the heavy technical processes of the computer world. I'm so glad you pushed me over the cliff to get my 62 mp camera – to use a teens phrase, it's simply awesome.

Both you Willy and your lovely partner Louise are a roll models for happiness within a partnership and your children are testament to the moral codes and values you uphold. I thank you for your friendship.

Photographic locations

The numbers below relate to the page number and the approximate geographical location of each photograph.

Simon Nevill

I'm a self-taught photographer, however my industrial design training has certainly helped my journey through the publishing and photographic world. Being a keen naturalist all my life has also given me a deep love and understanding of the natural sciences and hopefully this is reflected in my work. Having had many occupations throughout my life has shown me that you can achieve anything if the motivation and drive is there.

Now and then I receive wonderful emails regarding the various books I have published and the intrinsic rewards I derive from these letters make my journey even more worthwhile. I do hope you enjoy this photographic journey through this vast state.

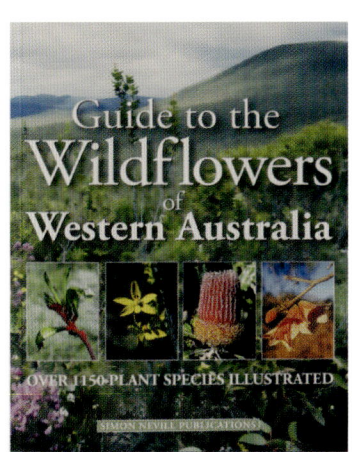

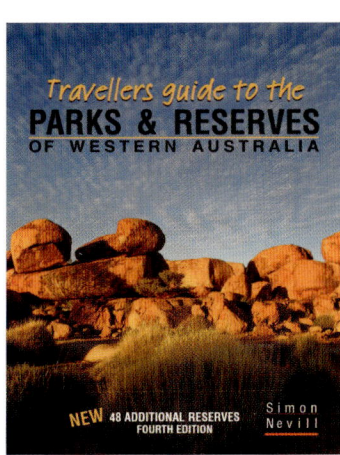

Guide to Wildflowers of Western Australia

Travellers Guide to the Parks and Reserves of Western Australia

Birds of Western Australia

Guide to the Wildlife of Perth and the South West

Perth and Fremantle Past and Present

All photographs in the Panorama book are by Simon Nevill and are available as large prints.

snpub@bigpond.net.au

75% of the pictures in this book are taken with 21 mp camera system and 25% with a 62 mp camera system.

All of Simon's books are available from the leading bookstores or online.   www.simonnevill.com

Published by Simon Nevill Publications
Email: snpub@bigpond.net.au

All photographs by Simon J. Nevill
© Copyright photographs and text
Simon J. Nevill 2015

The book is copyright. All rights reserved. No part of this publication may be reproduced, stored in a retrieval system or transmitted in any form or by any means, mechanical, electronic, photocopying, recording or otherwise without the consent of the publisher/author in writing.

National Library of Australia Cataloguing-in-Publication data
Title: Panorama Western Australia
ISBN 978-0-9923434-9-1
Panoramic photographs of Western Australia

Design concepts: Simon J. Nevill
Graphics: Leanne Quince, Graphics Above